The World Through My Glasses

Krisha Dhaduk

BookLeaf Publishing

Presentation by *BookLeaf Publishing*

Web: www.bookleafpub.com

E-mail: info@bookleafpub.com

ISBN: 9789357613620

First edition 2022

Let's Start!

Have you ever wanted to start...
A new life?
A new adventure?
New possibilities?
But started and stopped
Over and over again

Stuck in that rut
Can't go ahead no more
Try to get out
Try to think forward
Get that mindset straight
Come on, let's start again!

Our Love

A billion degrees in heat on the sun,
Yet, you warm up my heart the most.

Even if there's a fight, million-to-one,
You'd win, yet you wouldn't boast.

Your smile's brilliance could blind many,
Yet, there's no one you would hurt.

I watch as admirers surround you, plenty,
Your gentle, yet sharp facial features flirt.

I wish I could be by your side every day,
Yet, we are two rivers that flow parallel.

I want to make your acquaintance, I pray,
In this ball, I want to be your only belle.

Yet, we reside in separate levels of this game of
life,
My innocent hope that we could love without
strife.

Behind My Back

You little backstabber, you!
Coming up from behind,
With a camouflaged hue.

You are a foul hunter, you!
Shot me down with success,
You know well how to subdue.

I did not even sense it.
Why, you pierced into me,
Praise for this well-hidden skit.

The pain I feel is immense.
Radiating throughout,
It broke through my defense.

Your venom slowly seeps in.
That smooth toxic aura,
Flows in my body like gin.

I try to break through this phase.
Though I am now feeble,
I find ways to clear the haze.

Shock fills up my scattered thoughts.
I lose control over me.

Potent betrayal you brought.

I suffer from the results.
I keep looking back now.
Shivers from latent insults.

Congrats, you have broken me.
When I least expected,
I was pushed like a dummy.

You pinned me down with your tack,
Dumb me who could not see,
Got devastated from behind my back.

Older

Baby rattles and formula bottles,
Velvety diapers and constant gripers,
Those high feeding chairs and cute teddy bears,
Rocking horses and how-to-walk courses,
Those were simpler times.

Kindergarten and chocolate milk cartons,
Peaceful nap time and playing with gross slime,
Colorful book fair and glittery hair,
The alphabet and all that P.E. sweat,
I would reverse life.

Start middle school and trying to be cool,
Choose a lunch table and keep grades stable,
Many more classes and bathroom passes,
Spelling bee and locker-related glee,
It was more fun then.

Made it to high school, and there are less rules,
Fun football games and academic fame,
All those pep rallies and class assemblies,
Joining new clubs and go to the prom hub,
There's no going back.

I'm Sick of This!

As the smooth, cold syrup flows down my
throat,
I feel as if I'm sailing on a boat.
Far away from all this pain,
Especially the throbbing of my brain.

All the soreness from my raw, aching mouth,
Has dissolved by the pink liquid gone south.
Now I shall finally get better,
As predicted by the doctor's letter.

Though, as I sleep in peace,
The agony renews its lease.
It makes itself at home in me,
Ignoring my desperate plea.

I was too early; this all has yet to go,
So I have become quite the show.
My helpless kin watch silently,
As I thrust every which way violently.

My tired body has succumbed,
My organs have been drummed,
My mind has been benumbed,
My willpower has been crumbed.

Suffering

He watches as I wriggle in the chokehold,
Occasional glance or two, but no interest.
Looks like he's the Devil's VIP guest,
Instead of liquid gold, evil fills his mold.

He covers his mouth with his cold hands,
I see a peak of his inhuman grin.
Millions of goosebumps raise on my pale skin,
As I realized, I fell and could no more stand.

I watched blankly as he caressed my face,
A smile so rotten shown, it reeked of arrogance.
I wished to push him away, a frightening dance,
His sadistic spite crushes my feeble love like a
mace.

I'm an eyewitness to his leaving me behind,
Yet his brilliant love has truly left me blind.

From Your Bed

Dearest user, are you nuts?!
I should be used for sleep.
As it is, I frequently look at your butt.
You certainly do your tasks in heaps.

You used me to cry your heart out,
You used me to do homework on,
In my blanket, you gave muffled shouts,
In me, you hid and watched videos 'til dawn.

I cried in pain as you jumped on me,
I sat and read your books along with you,
I drank in the silence as you sipped tea,
I winced as you loudly suffered from flu.

I laughed as your friends gave you gossip,
I looked away as you glared at me for messy
hair,
I got annoyed when, on me, you spilled guac
dip,
I reflected as you recited aloud your prayers.

We have had quite an interesting life together,
At the end of the day, I lull you to sleep,
You lay on me as light as a feather,
I push you to your dreams, slowly down deep.

I Am a Fool

I complete others' homework because I enjoy it.

And I say "OK" when the popular girls ask me
to sit.
My skirt went from long to short with a huge
slit.

Addicted to hearing compliments, don't know
when to quit.

Fell down from these dumb high heels, and my
skirt split.
Oh dear, I am a puppet whose string is held by
others' mitts.
Objection! Why do I have to change to fit?
Lets leave all this! Away from here, I see a
future brightly lit.

Sweet Dreams

Standing on the beach with moonlit smiles,
We hold each other as the waves cleanse our
sins.
Even if our families came to divide,
Even if a tsunami took us beneath the tides,
The love we have will stay in the history books.

Daring us to unite stood our enemies from
behind.
Revealing their evil intent, they flash towards us.
Even if we are pulled apart, a heart is imperfect
without two halves.
All the tears we shed mix in with the ocean's
salty swell.
May we get together undisputed in our sleep,
Sweet dreams, my love.

She

It eats away at me like a parasite.
I know I shouldn't, but she deserves a bite.
With her eyes so bright and her teeth so white,
Slowly, in me, I feel my will rise with spite.

She sways her hips and winks with charm,
Multiple boys stick onto her dainty arms.
To all her teachers, she shows that slick smarm,
Now tell me, why shouldn't I think of harm?

Enough is enough! Just done with it all,
Today, she wore her skirt and fluffy shawl.
What's even worse? She'll draw all appall.
She kissed her friend's man, leading to a brawl.

Exasperated, I looked at the commotion,
Students rowdily waved around like the ocean.
From the sight of this all, I moved towards a
notion,
That, from now on, I should ignore envy with
devotion.

Different Doors

I'm bored of this routine.
I have regressed to a dingy robot.
Unless…

What if I left the room I'm in?
What if there are others out there?

I gingerly close this door,
And run across the threshold of another.

Where am I?
I look diagonally at a silent crowd.
They sit in a semi-circle hidden by the dark.
From the swanlike pose I'm stiffened into,
I bend my feet and lift up in an airy bubble.
Floating and drifting as if the ground isn't
satisfactory.
I swiftly flew across these polished floors,
As the crowd roared in encore.
My delicate tutu reverberated with my feat,
As I bowed to my admirers.

I must say, it's time to move on.
We shouldn't stay stuck in this dream.

As I exited the path of a dance extraordinaire,

I tripped and fell, pushing open a new door.

My sight cleared up to a bright blue sky.
Thankful to be outside,
I stared around.
Yuck! Something wet beheld my cheek!
I turned to glance into the snout of a mare.
As stunningly brown as my decaf espresso,
I brushed its mane and fed it apples.
I must say, there are many animals around.
Handsome horses and spirited chickens,
Pale pink pigs and jaded cows…
Is this what farm life is like?
I walked forwards, satisfied with my travels.

But I feel as if a blanket of homesickness is on
me…

As I return, that routine may bore me to death,
Yet, nothing could beat home.

Blink

With you, I feel at home.
With you, I need not to roam.
You are my destination,
You are my every sensation.

Even if I'm wrongly blinded,
I know you won't be close-minded.
Even if my faith in you shrinks,
You'll be there when I blink.

Stay

We have a connection stronger than steel,
Leaving you behind would be a no-deal.
You are my strength; I won't ever let you cry,
Even if that means I have to pluck every star
from the sky.

You may not be close to me,
But distance can't take away my key.
You're my key to happiness every day,
Of each moment we spend, I do a replay.

You shine on the outside,
You burn on the inside,
Your hard work won't go in vain,
I will help pave your lane.

Even if, to countless, we become prey,
Know this, by your side, I will always stay.

Strange

Why are you avoiding my eyes?
Is it because you have a bunch of lies?
What's the purpose of your awful disguise?
I do not get you; I must not be wise.

When you gaze at me, you gaze past me,
And for me, you are the only one I see.
I thought once we were together, we'd be free.
Yet, I feel that we are trapped together to some
degree.

Silence floats around you, filled with hesitation,
I'm beginning to doubt the existence of our
relation.
For I have noticed that you have shunned
communication.
Which is beginning to lead to our love's
separation.

One day you show up, the next day you're gone,
I'm slowly understanding this line you have
drawn.
Hour by hour, it seems to me you are the Devil's
spawn.
I can't stay near anymore; I'm starting anew at
dawn.

Mother Nature

The eclectic mix of colors on those giant oak
trees,
Attracts the likeness of those energetic buzzing
bees.

As they cheerfully step onto the half-fresh,
half-senescent grass,
Carefree families set up their portable, pretty
picnics and amass.

Kids gleefully run on the hills, their feet
crunching on the fallen leaves.
Parents rest up under the shade of the oaks; the
peace, to them, relieves.

Lovers slept, hands together, in a patch of
satiny-smooth petunias.
The dogs' barking and the wind's wispy jingling
make a fanciful fantasia.

Fresh, earthy scents rise up amidst the miniature,
swampy grove.
A father and son stop to chew on some juicy
gooseberries, leaving their rove.

Nature's serenity brings about peace absent in
peoples' busy lives.
One can only hope that nature's embrace is what
we need to thrive.

Autumnal Mood

A time to cuddle
Nature's way of letting go
Let all the leaves fall.

Stand Out

Separating from the like-minded crowd
Telling off haters who say, "You can't fit in"
Accepting differences that others laugh at
Never giving in to mass conformity
Don't cover yourself up for anyone else

Open up to others as books can't be read when
closed
Underneath your disguise, your true identity
can't shine
To be successful, you need to stand out from
everyone else

Where Are They?!

I look frantically left and right,
Knowing I wouldn't see at night.
I check under the couch with caution,
Knowing I would wreck everything if not done.

I search the cobwebby crevices of cabinets,
Only to realize that the short height is to my
head a threat.
I carefully back out to avoid hitting my noggin.
Yet, I press my butt on my laptop and
involuntarily log-in.

I feel around my desk for their distinct shape,
Disappointingly, all I get is a worn-out piece of
tape.
I annoyingly try to flick the tape off my finger,
But I hit my hand on my desk, only pain will
linger.

I finger gently through my pockets,
Waiting for that sigh of relief to rocket.
I pat down yesterday's jacket,
Only to find a small pretzel packet.

Mom was right; I am way too clumsy,
I wish I kept them right with my mumsy.

She didn't ever lose them; she's such a role
model,
Yet, the thing I do best is a gait with a toddle.

I give up! I will just tape the door close instead.
I can't even find things, I'm such a bonehead.
I hug the Honda SUV before I leave for the
night,
When something flashed in my eyes, a reflection
of light.

I reached for where the light came from,
But it's the roof of the car…why from there
would it come?
I felt something hard and sharp but very familiar.
To confirm, with my fingers, I traced around
their spurs.

I FINALLY FOUND THEM! MY CAR KEYS!
Self-assuredly, I shall keep them closer as I give
them a squeeze.

Music is Healing

Music is healing
The sounds to soothe the soul
Put you to sleep
Get you on your feet
That little song
That little tune
That little melody
Mutes all illness

Music is medicine
It's healing for the mind
It's for the heart
It's for the spirit
It's for you and me
Feel the rhythm
Coursing through bodies
Heal the world
Heal us all
Heal us, Music

Just Dance

Dance
You move your arms and legs
You dance like no one is watching
So many moves, so many sounds
Other dancers envy your magic
You dance away your troubles
You dance away your fears
You dance away your sorrow
You dance away your pain
Your elegance is beyond compare
You are not compressed
You let your worries float away
The beat takes you higher
You don't want to ever come down
Dance the night away
Dance until the day ends
Dance is life's rhythm
You keep moving
You keep going
Dance

All Good Things Must Come to An End

Time goes by so fast
In a blink of an eye
And everything is over
Everything in life
Whether good or bad
Everything has a time
When everything ends
Nothing is left
Just memories